DATE DUE			
APR 21 1995			
APR 2 1 1997			
FEB 2 4 1998			
MAR 1 8 1998			
MAR 2 3 1999			
MAR 2 4 1999			
APR 2 7 1999			
NOV 1 7 1999			
MAR 2 9 2000			
MAY 2 0 2001			
MAR 0 6 2002			
MAY 1 5 2002			
NOV 2 0 2002			
MAR 2 8 2012			

DEMCO NO. 38-298

FACTS AMERICA

PRESIDENTS
OF THE UNITED STATES

RICHARD O'NEILL AND ANTONIA D. BRYAN

SMITHMARK

About the authors

Richard O'Neill has been a soldier, boxer, laborer, actor, and writer of fiction, comic strips, and stage and television plays. In recent years, he has specialized in writing historical nonfiction. Mr. O'Neill is the author of *Suicide Squads: Special Attack Weapons of World War II* and has co-authored two books on toy collecting. He was a major contributor to *Lands and Peoples*, a multivolume work published in the United States in 1990/91.

Antonia Bryan has been a free-lance writer for 25 years, with an emphasis on educational publishing and museum collections. She writes in many media for all ages, on topics ranging from American history to human values, creative writing, Japanese art, and the environment. She also brings up two children in New York City.

Editor:
Philip de Ste. Croix

Designer:
Stonecastle Graphics Ltd

Picture research:
Leora Kahn

Coordinating editors:
Andrew Preston
Kristen Schilo

Production:
Ruth Arthur
Sally Connolly
Neil Randles
Andrew Whitelaw

Production editor:
Didi Charney

Director of production:
Gerald Hughes

Typesetter:
Pagesetters Incorporated

Color and monochrome reproduction:
Advance Laser Graphic Arts, Hong Kong

Printed and bound in Hong Kong by
Leefung-Asco Printers Ltd

Text copyright © 1992 SMITHMARK
Publishers Inc./Richard O'Neill

1992 Colour Library Books Ltd
Godalming Business Centre
Woolsack Way, Godalming
Surrey GU7 1XW, United Kingdom
CLB 2603

This edition published in 1992 by
SMITHMARK Publishers Inc.
112 Madison Avenue
New York, NY 10016 USA

SMITHMARK books are available for bulk purchase for sales promotion and premium use. For details, write or call the manager of special sales, SMITHMARK Publishers Inc., 112 Madison Avenue, New York, NY 10016; (212) 532-6600.

Library of Congress Cataloging-in-Publication Data

O'Neill, Richard.
    Facts America. Presidents of the United States / Richard O'Neill
& Antonia D. Bryan.
        p. cm.
    Includes bibliographical references and index.
    Summary: Discusses the lives, achievements, and times of the forty
men who have been elected to the highest office in the United
States.
    ISBN 0-8317-2310-6 (hardcover)
    1. Presidents—United States—Biography—Juvenile literature.
[1. Presidents.] I. Bryan, Antonia D., 1946–   II. Title.
III. Title: Presidents of the United States.
E176.1.054   1992
973'.0992—dc20
    [B]   92-9401

The inauguration of President John F. Kennedy took place on January 21, 1961. Here, he is leaving the White House for the ceremony at the Capitol in the company of outgoing President Dwight D. Eisenhower.

Contents

1 The Founding Fathers   4

2 Expanding Horizons   10

3 The Struggle for Union   20

4 Reconstruction and Industry   26

5 World Conflict and a New Century   36

6 Modern America   48

1 The Founding Fathers

George Washington, the first president of the American nation, was born in 1732. His family was one of the oldest in Virginia, where his great-grandfather had settled in 1656. At the age of 21, Washington fought heroically in the French and Indian War, which raged in Canada. He emerged angered by the British officers' scorn for American-born soldiers. Back home, a wealthy colonial landowner, he was strongly against Britain's unfair taxes and land laws, and became more and more active in resisting British rule. When the revolutionary war began in 1775, the Continental Congress chose this upright and dignified Virginian as commander in chief of the Continental army. He refused payment for the job.

During the Revolution, Washington seldom had more than 10,000 men. Untrained, ragged, and poorly armed, many deserted. But his remarkable strength of character kept his frozen and hungry soldiers from giving up in the bitter winter of 1777/78, when he shared their hardships at Valley Forge. In October 1781, Washington trapped the main British force at Yorktown. They surrendered, and the fighting was over.

After the war, Washington went home to Mount Vernon, refusing to become dictator of the new republic. In 1787, he agreed to oversee the historic convention that resulted in the U.S. Constitution. On the Constitution's approval, the "father of his country" was elected president, taking office in April 1789. His first act was to work for the Bill of Rights. He was elected again in 1792. No one ran against him.

Washington belonged to no political party, for he wanted to be fair to all Americans. His concern was the good of the country. In his farewell speech of 1796, he warned against states arguing between each other and urged caution in forming ties with foreign powers. He flatly refused requests to run for a third term. Washington died of a throat infection in December 1799.

George Washington   (*in office 1789–97*)

◀ *This portrait of Washington shows him as stern and serious. He was respected rather than loved, but at the time of his death, one of his generals praised him for being "first in war, first in peace, first in the hearts of his countrymen."*

▲ *Sulgrave Manor, now a museum, in Northamptonshire, England, was the home of Washington's ancestors from 1539 until 1610. Washington's family has been traced back to 1260, when it was called "de Wessington."*

◀ *Washington's army spent the freezing winter of 1777/78 at Valley Forge, near Philadelphia, which the British had captured. They had little food, shelter, or clothing. Here, Washington and his French ally, the marquis de Lafayette, walk among the men to give them courage.*

▲ *A famous story relates how Washington, as a boy, admitted chopping down his father's cherry tree, with the words "Father, I cannot tell a lie." The tale was probably invented to show the great man's love of truth.*

▼ *On the night of December 25, 1776, Washington led 2,500 men across the icy Delaware River to attack the Hessians (Germans in British service) at Trenton, New Jersey. Drunk on Christmas liquor, the Hessians were surprised, and some 900 were captured. Washington lost only 5 men.*

John Adams (1797–1801)

John Adams, second president, was born in Quincy, Massachusetts, in 1735. A brilliant student at Harvard University, he became one of the top lawyers in Boston and spoke out against unfair British taxation. In 1775, Adams led the Second Continental Congress in forming the minutemen (militia) of New England into the Continental army; he also appointed Washington commander in chief. Adams headed the Board of War during the Revolution. In 1776, he dominated the heated debates in Congress that resulted in the Declaration of Independence. He wrote most of the Massachusetts state constitution himself. It would serve as a pattern for other states.

Adams spent the years 1780 to 1788 as a diplomat in Europe. He got Holland to recognize the United States and served as the first U.S. minister to Great Britain. On his return, he was elected Washington's vice president, the first man to hold what he himself called a "most insignificant office."

Adams was nominated as the Federalist candidate for the presidency in 1796, narrowly beating Thomas Jefferson. When U.S. merchant ships were blocked by French revolutionaries, many Americans called for war with the slogan "Millions for defense, but not one cent for tribute!" Adams strengthened the U.S. Navy but lost popularity by standing strongly for peace.

In 1800, the government moved from Philadelphia to Washington, D.C., where the Adams family found the half-finished White House very uncomfortable. Later the same year, Adams was defeated by Thomas Jefferson and retired to a life of study and writing with his wife, Abigail, also a talented writer.

Adams lived longer than any other U.S. president. He died on July 4, 1826, the same day as his friend and rival Jefferson.

Adams believed that the job of the ▶ government was to keep people happy, but that the support of the people was what made that possible. Thomas Jefferson felt that Adams was so important in forming the new nation that he called him "the colossus of independence."

▼ The White House was first known as the Presidential Palace. It was unfinished when Adams moved in. The famous north portico with its half circle of columns was not added until the 1820s.

The 44-gun frigate USS ▶ Constitution (seen here after a battle with the British warship Guerrière in 1812) was launched in 1797. She was nicknamed Old Ironsides because of the strength of her oak timbers.

◀ In the Boston Massacre of 1770, British troops fired on angry citizens, killing five. Adams spoke out against mob violence and in court successfully defended British soldiers charged with murder.

▲ Peacefield, in Quincy, Massachusetts, was better known as the Old House. It was bought by Adams in 1788 and remodeled by his capable wife, Abigail. He died there in 1826.

Thomas Jefferson (1801–9)

Thomas Jefferson, third president, was born on his family's plantation in Albemarle County, Virginia, in 1743. He dedicated his life to the pursuit of freedom for his nation and its individual citizens. Jefferson was the main author of the Declaration of Independence, his finest monument. He drew it up, working with John Adams and Benjamin Franklin, as a delegate to the Second Continental Congress in 1776. He did not fight in the Revolution, however, but aided Washington while serving as governor of Virginia from 1779 to 1781.

Elected to Congress in 1783, Jefferson was responsible for simplifying the money system and for new land laws. He returned from service as minister to France (1785–89) to become Washington's secretary of state. In 1796, Jefferson became vice president under John Adams. In 1800, he was elected president by a narrow margin but easily won reelection in 1804.

Jefferson believed that "the best government is the least government," and he kept America out of the Napoleonic Wars. Jeffersonian democracy came to stand for freedom of speech and religion, and for the rights of individual states rather than authority centered in the federal government. Under Jefferson, taxes were cut and slaves could no longer be brought into the country. In 1803, the Louisiana Purchase almost doubled the size of the United States. The 530 million acres of land cost about three cents each.

Jefferson refused to seek reelection in 1808 and retired to Monticello, an elegant mansion he himself had designed. Here, among the lovely gardens he also had created, he pursued a wide range of interests, from philosophy and architecture to natural history. His many inventions included a decoding machine, a polygraph (for copying handwriting), a swivel chair, and an improved plow. Jefferson himself believed that his finest deed was the foundation of the University of Virginia in 1819. He died on July 4, 1826, the 50th anniversary of the Declaration of Independence.

▲ The Declaration of Independence was drawn up by a committee, but Jefferson was its primary author. Left to right: Jefferson, Roger Sherman, Benjamin Franklin, Robert Livingston, and John Adams.

◀ Rembrandt Peale's portrait of Jefferson captures the humor and intelligence of the "man of the people." It was completed during Jefferson's presidency.

▲ This engraving shows the many sides of Jefferson's genius. The statesman is revealed by the globe on the floor and the Declaration of Independence he points to proudly; the statue and books show him as a writer and thinker; and on a stand beside him is one of his many inventions. Jefferson was so wise, he became known as the "sage of Monticello."

◀ Jefferson himself designed Monticello, his magnificent mansion near Charlottesville, Virginia. As one of the earliest and finest examples of American classical revival architecture, it has been preserved by a Memorial Trust since the 1920s, attracting many thousands of visitors every year.

2 Expanding Horizons *James Madison (1809–17)*

James Madison, fourth president, was born in Port Conway, Virginia, in 1751. He is called "the father of the Constitution," because he played such an important part in forming that document. Later, he drew up the Bill of Rights. Jefferson chose Madison as his secretary of state and supported him for president in 1808.

During Madison's first term, France and Britain preyed on American shipping, and he led the United States to war with Britain in June 1812. But the war went badly, and hardships of ordinary Americans were contrasted with the lavish parties given by Madison's popular young wife, Dolley, who served a new delicacy, ice cream. When the British burned the White House in 1814, Madison barely escaped. But the following year, the war ended, and his popularity bounced back. By 1816, he could be certain of the election of his friend James Monroe. Madison died in 1836, the last president who had been a Founding Father, a member of the Constitutional Convention.

◀ James Madison was sickly and only five foot two. Washington Irving, who wrote The Legend of Sleepy Hollow, noted that, standing beside his tall, stately wife, Dolley, Madison was just "poor Jeemy . . . a withered little apple-john."

The original manuscript ▶ of the "The Star-Spangled Banner," by lawyer and poet Francis Scott Key. It quickly became a popular song but was not made the official national anthem until 1931.

◀ Dolley Payne Madison was famous for her hospitality. She served her husband and the widower Thomas Jefferson as White House hostess.

In the War of 1812, Francis Scott ▶ Key watched the British bombard Fort McHenry, near Baltimore. It inspired his "The Star-Spangled Banner."

James Monroe (1817–25)

John C. Calhoun, who spoke for the slaveholding Southern states, was Monroe's secretary of war and became John Quincy Adams's vice president.

James Monroe, fifth president, was born in Westmoreland County, Virginia, in 1758. After serving gallantly in the revolutionary war, he studied law under Thomas Jefferson. Monroe became President Jefferson's ablest diplomat—in 1803, he negotiated the Louisiana Purchase, buying some 828,000 square miles of the Mississippi Valley from France for $15 million. Under Madison, Monroe served as secretary of state and secretary for war, then easily won the presidential elections of both 1816 and 1820.

His presidency, called the Era of Good Feelings, was marked by progress, prosperity, and peace. His greatest legacy was the Monroe Doctrine of 1823, encouraging European nations to keep their hands off the American continent and promising that the United States would stay out of European quarrels. Monroe paid little attention to personal business, however, and died almost penniless on July 4, 1831.

▼ As the last of the revolutionary war heroes to gain high office, Monroe has been nicknamed "the last cocked hat."

▼ The president uses a globe to explain to his cabinet the Monroe Doctrine, designed to keep Europe from interfering in the revolt of Spanish colonies in Latin America.

John Quincy Adams (1825–29)

John Quincy Adams, sixth president, was born in Braintree (now Quincy), Massachusetts, in 1767. As a child, he watched the famous revolutionary battle at Bunker Hill. The eldest son of John Adams, he was the only president's child also to become president. From the age of 11, Adams worked as his father's secretary on diplomatic missions to Europe and, at 14, became private secretary to the American minister to Russia. By the time he went to Harvard University, he already spoke seven languages.

For a short time, Adams was a Boston lawyer, but in 1794, he was appointed minister to Holland, and later to Russia and Prussia. In 1803, he entered the U.S. Senate as a Federalist, but his support for President Jefferson annoyed Massachusetts Federalists and he had to resign. Adams served further in Europe but was brought back by President Monroe in 1817 to be his secretary of state. Under Monroe, he arranged to buy Florida from Spain and played an important role in formulating the Monroe Doctrine.

In 1824, Adams was one of five presidential candidates. He won by a narrow margin. Adams considered himself above politics and refused to work to gain support. As a result, his plans to improve communications and education did not succeed, and he felt he had failed as president. In the 1828 election, he was heavily defeated by the colorful Andrew Jackson.

Elected to Congress in 1830, Adams worked hard against slavery, speaking so well that he was nicknamed Old Man Eloquent. In 1848, he collapsed from a stroke in the House of Representatives and died in the Speaker's Room soon after. He was 80 years old and had served during 11 presidencies.

▲ This picture of John Quincy Adams late in life is based on a photograph. The first successful photograph ever made was taken in France in 1826, when Adams was president.

▼ Adams was dignified and serious. In spite of his small build and high voice, he was a brilliant speaker.

Noah Webster worked for ▶ *20 years on his famous dictionary. It included 12,000 words never before in a dictionary and was published in 1828.*

▲ *A formal White House ball given in 1824 by Adams's wife, Louisa. She was often sick but tried to do her job as her husband's hostess. At the left, President Adams stands with his hand relaxed inside his jacket; in the center is the next president, Andrew Jackson.*

◀ *Adams went to college at Harvard, America's oldest university, founded in 1636. This is how it looked about 1810. When Adams arrived at the age of 18, he was already an experienced diplomat.*

Andrew Jackson (1829–37)

Tall and slim, Andrew ▶ *Jackson presents an imposing figure in this portrait of him as president. Often in pain from old wounds and suffering from tuberculosis, he remained active to the last, riding horseback every day.*

Andrew Jackson, seventh president, was the child of Irish immigrants, born in the Carolinas in 1767 on what was then the western frontier. Although known for gambling and fighting duals, he became a leading lawyer in Tennessee, which elected him its first congressman in 1796. He also served as senator for a short time and became a respected judge.

In the War of 1812, Jackson's toughness earned him the nickname Old Hickory. His Tennessee militia crushed the pro-British Creek tribe at Horseshoe Bend in March 1814; and the following January, he led 6,000 backwoods troops to defeat 12,000 British soldiers in the battle of New Orleans. Jackson had become a national hero.

Jackson ran for president in 1824 and almost won. But in 1828, he swept to power as "the people's choice" and was elected again in 1832. His presidency was marked by a battle with the Bank of the United States, which he ruined by withdrawing federal money and putting it in state banks. But his respect for states' rights did not stop him from sending U.S. troops into South Carolina when that state threatened to leave the Union over high taxes on foreign goods. In 1836, he recognized the republic of Texas. He was the first president to ride on a train, and the first to survive an assassination attempt.

Jackson did not always handle money matters well; he introduced the spoils system, rewarding political supporters with government jobs; and he seized land from Native Americans, causing enormous suffering. Yet his readiness to take action did much to set up the modern powers of the presidency. He died in 1845, partly from old wounds.

Raised on the rough frontier ▶ *of the Carolinas, Jackson was the first of seven presidents to be born in a log cabin.*

▼ Jackson was made a major general in the U.S. Army in 1814, after his Tennessee militia wiped out a force of Creek Native Americans.

▲ As a teenage captive in the revolutionary war, Jackson refused to clean a British officer's boots. He was scarred for life by the man's sword.

▼ Mounted on a white horse, Jackson rallies his men at the battle of New Orleans. His defeat of a larger British force made him a national hero.

Martin Van Buren (1837–41)

Martin Van Buren, eighth president, was born in Kinderhook, New York, in 1782. He was the first president born a U.S. citizen. As a senator, he led the formation of the Democratic party under Andrew Jackson and became Jackson's vice president in 1832.

With Jackson's support, Van Buren was elected president in 1836. But soon after he took office, the Panic of 1837 began a depression that lasted four years, earning him the nickname Martin Van Ruin. Northerners complained that he protected slavery, but Southerners blamed him for not forcing Texas, slave territory, into the Union.

The son of an innkeeper, Van Buren was a self-made man. But he lost the presidency in 1840, when he was unfairly called rich with little concern for ordinary people. He lost again when nominated as an anti-slavery candidate in 1848. He died supporting the Union cause during the Civil War, in 1862.

▼ *In 1837, Samuel Morse gave up a successful career as an artist to devote himself to science. Soon after, he developed Morse code, in which long and short signals stand for letters and numbers. He used it to send messages over the first electric telegraph line.*

▼ *Martin Van Buren was such a good politician that he was called "the little magician."*

Van Buren became the subject of cruel cartoons, such as this one, when he failed to solve the financial crisis of 1837. ▲

William Henry Harrison (March–April 1841)

This Shawnee uprising was a result of the white settlement Harrison encouraged as governor of Indiana Territory. In 1811, at Tippecanoe Creek, Harrison calmly led his militia to victory over a larger Native American force under the great chief Tecumseh.

Although Harrison came ▶ from a wealthy Virginia family, the Whig party promoted him as the "common man" candidate in 1840. Voters were won over by generous helpings of free hard cider.

William Henry Harrison ▶ came to fame as a soldier. He was 67 years old when he won his short-lived presidency. Only Ronald Reagan, in 1980, was older when elected president.

William Henry Harrison, ninth president, held office for only 30 days. Born on his family's Virginia plantation in 1773, he studied medicine at college but left for an army career. In 1800, Harrison was appointed governor of Indiana Territory, where he crushed a Native American uprising at Tippecanoe. He went on to fight heroically in the War of 1812.

Harrison's political career relied on his military reputation. His 1840 presidential campaign featured mass rallies and a rousing slogan: "Tippecanoe and Tyler, too!" Tyler was his little-known running mate. In spite of Harrison's aristocratic upbringing, he was portrayed as a frontiersman who drank hard cider while his opponent, President Van Buren, sipped champagne. Harrison won, then delivered his long inaugural address outdoors, on a wet winter's day in 1841. He caught cold and, a month later, died of pneumonia in the White House. In 1889, his grandson, Benjamin Harrison, also became president.

John Tyler (1841–45)

John Tyler, tenth president, was born in Charles City County, Virginia, in 1790. Tyler served as congressman, senator, and governor of Virginia before being chosen as William Henry Harrison's vice president. On Harrison's death in 1841, Tyler became the first vice president to take over after a president had died in office.

Tyler was fiercely independent. He used the veto, his presidential power to reject a bill passed by Congress, against his supporters. His party kicked him out, making him the only acting president ever without one. In 1844, he decided not to run.

In 1861, Tyler led a peace mission to Washington from the Southern states, which were deadlocked with the North over the issue of slavery. When the mission failed, he supported Southern withdrawal from the Union. He was elected to the Confederate House of Representatives just before his death in 1862.

▼ Tyler was noted for his politeness, but his rigid independence turned even his own party against him. His cabinet of advisers resigned while he was in office.

Camped beside their covered wagon, pioneers take their evening meal on the prairie. Tyler's term of office saw the Great Migration of 1842–43 when many settlers moved west along the Oregon Trail. ▲

▲ President Tyler was born in this frame house on his family's Greenway estate, in Charles City County, Virginia. He studied law under his father, who was governor of Virginia from 1808 to 1811.

◄ Julia Gardner Tyler became John Tyler's second wife in 1844. His first wife had died in 1842. Tyler was the first president to marry while in office.

James Knox Polk (1845–49)

James Knox Polk, 11th president, was born in Mecklenburg County, North Carolina, in 1795. His support for Andrew Jackson was so strong that he was called Young Hickory and won Jackson's old seat in Congress eight times. As the Democratic candidate in 1844, Polk narrowly won. He ignored the issue of slavery but totally supported expansion across the American West.

As president, Polk accepted the 49th parallel as the official border between Oregon and Canada, even though his campaign slogan had been "54–40 or fight!" But he failed to settle arguments with Mexico over land, resulting in war in May 1846. After the United States' victory in 1848, a peace treaty added the areas of Texas, California, and the southwestern states to the nation, over a million square miles of territory.

Polk announced that he would only serve one term and did not allow his advisers to waste time campaigning. He accomplished almost everything he said he would when he took office. Overwork may have contributed to his death soon after leaving the White House in 1849.

The promise of easy riches ▶ brought thousands to California in the gold rush of 1842. In 1846, "Polk's war" won the territory from Mexico.

▼ *After winning the battle of Chapultepec in the Mexican War, General Winfield Scott enters Mexico City peacefully in September 1847.*

▲ *Polk was cold, forbidding, and generally unpopular, but his support for manifest destiny, the idea that gaining western lands was noble and right, resulted in the greatest territorial expansion in America's history.*

3 The Struggle for Union *Zachary Taylor (1849–50)*

Zachary Taylor, 12th president, was born in Orange County, Virginia, in 1784. He had little education and no political experience, but proved a brave soldier against Native Americans and the British in the War of 1812. His men called him Old Rough and Ready because he scorned fine uniforms. They named his rival, the neat and demanding General Winfield Scott, Old Fuss and Feathers.

In the Mexican War, Taylor got credit for victories won mostly through the skill of junior officers. He accepted the nomination in 1848 and beat Democratic and Free Soil (anti-slavery) candidates. Although he owned slaves, he was against laws that he felt favored the pro-slavery South, and threatened to use troops against any Southern rebellion. Taylor died of a stomach complaint after only 16 months in office, in 1850. Some felt that his death had saved the Union.

▼ *Zachary Taylor, who never cast a vote himself, won election as a hero of the Mexican War. When pro-slavery states threatened revolt, he showed the same stubborn courage he had had in battle.*

With a spyglass to his eye, ▶ Taylor looks over the hard-won field of Buena Vista, where his 5,000 troops defeated some 16,000 Mexicans in February 1847.

▼ Zachary Taylor in the uniform of a major general. In his 40 years as a soldier, he fought the British, the Sauk, Fox, and Seminole tribes, and the Mexicans.

Millard Fillmore (1850–53)

▲ In the 1850s, engines such as this one hauled passengers and freight over the great rail network that was fast connecting all parts of the nation.

UNCLE TOM'S CABIN

UNCLE TOM & EVA.

▲ Harriet Beecher Stowe's anti-slavery novel Uncle Tom's Cabin first came out as a serial. It sold 300,000 copies in 1852, the year it was published in book form.

▼ President Millard Fillmore's successful attempt to preserve the Union by a compromise on slavery cost him renomination in 1852.

Millard Fillmore, 13th president, was born in Locke, New York, in 1800. He was raised in a log cabin and apprenticed to a cloth maker. Too poor to attend college, he worked hard for enough education to become a successful lawyer and politician. In 1848, he was nominated vice president to widen the appeal of Zachary Taylor, a slave-owning Southerner.

Fillmore became president on Taylor's sudden death in 1850. By supporting the Compromise of 1850, which Taylor had opposed, he delayed the Civil War. The compromise outlawed slavery in Washington, D.C., admitted California to the Union as a free state, and let New Mexico and Utah decide for themselves. But to get Southern states to agree, the compromise introduced the Fugitive Slave Law, forcing anti-slavers to help return runaway slaves to their owners. Fillmore's support for this law cost him renomination in 1852, and in 1856, he also gained few votes as candidate for the anti-immigrant American party, the Know-Nothings. During the Civil War, he supported the Union but disliked Abraham Lincoln. He died in 1874.

Franklin Pierce (1853–57)

Franklin Pierce, 14th president, was born in Hillsboro, New Hampshire, in 1804. Pierce trained as a lawyer, then served as a general in the Mexican War. As a Democrat in 1852, Pierce easily beat General Winfield Scott, who had been his commanding officer. Pierce was handsome, a fine speaker, and, at 48, the youngest man elected president so far. But there was sadness in his life—all three of his young sons died, the last in a train crash on the way to Washington for his father's inauguration.

Pierce supported the Compromise of 1850 and approved laws letting territories decide if they would allow slavery. As a result, war nearly broke out in Kansas. In 1856, Pierce's own party refused to let him run for president again. When the Civil War came, his stand against freeing the slaves made New Englanders so angry they attacked him. Pierce died in New Hampshire, depressed and forgotten, in 1869.

▼ *Franklin Pierce tried to please those for slavery and those against it. He was rejected by his party in 1856.*

▲ *In Kansas, those against slavery celebrated when laws allowing slavery were removed.*

In 1853, Commodore ▶ *Matthew Perry first impressed the Japanese by boldly anchoring four U.S. ships in Tokyo Bay, which was forbidden to foreigners. His visit opened that country to trade with the West.*

James Buchanan (1857–61)

◀ *James Buchanan was indecisive. He was accused of being for the South, but when war came immediately after his term, he gave President Lincoln his full support.*

▲ *Federal troops storm the U.S. arsenal at Harpers Ferry, occupied by anti-slavery militants under John Brown in October 1859. Brown was found guilty of treason and hanged.*

James Buchanan, 15th president, was born near Mercersburg, Pennsylvania, in 1791. A successful lawyer and diplomat, he worked out the first American trade agreement with Russia. He served as secretary of state under James Polk.

In 1856, the Democrats were looking for a candidate who would not stir up passions about slavery. They chose Buchanan because he had no strong views on the subject. Even so, during his presidency, the nation became more and more divided. In 1860, he was not renominated, and Republican Abraham Lincoln won the election. Buchanan was relieved to step down. The Civil War began just weeks after he left office.

Buchanan vowed never to marry after the woman he was engaged to died, perhaps taking her own life. As president, his judgment was not good, and he made poor decisions in a difficult time. The day before he died, in 1868, he declared that history would prove his worth. He was wrong.

▼ *Dred Scott was a runaway slave, who declared himself free after living on "free soil." The Supreme Court ruled against him, a decision Buchanan felt would end controversy, but it outraged those against slavery.*

Abraham Lincoln (1861–65)

Abraham Lincoln, 16th president, was born in a log cabin near Hodgenville, Kentucky, in 1809. Raised on the wild Indiana frontier, he went to school for less than a year but learned to read and write. In 1831, Lincoln settled in Illinois, where he taught himself law, walking as far as 20 miles to get books. He served in the state government and became a successful lawyer in Springfield.

Lincoln joined the new Republican party in 1856 and two years later became famous for attacking slavery in his debates with Democratic senator Stephen A. Douglas. Lincoln's passionate speeches won him the nomination in 1860. He was elected the first Republican president by a large majority. In protest, South Carolina left the Union and soon joined with ten other Southern slave states to form their own nation, the Confederate States of America. On April 12, 1861, the Civil War began.

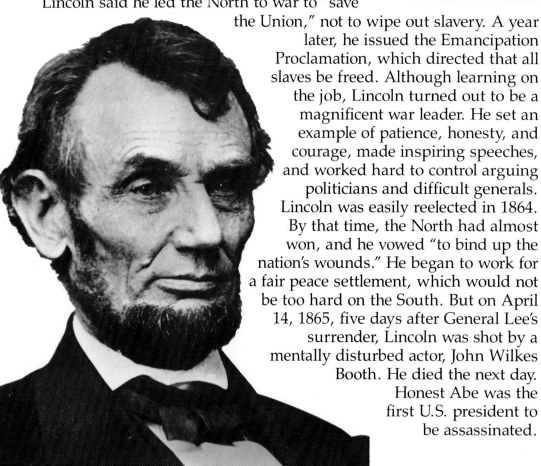

Lincoln said he led the North to war to "save the Union," not to wipe out slavery. A year later, he issued the Emancipation Proclamation, which directed that all slaves be freed. Although learning on the job, Lincoln turned out to be a magnificent war leader. He set an example of patience, honesty, and courage, made inspiring speeches, and worked hard to control arguing politicians and difficult generals. Lincoln was easily reelected in 1864. By that time, the North had almost won, and he vowed "to bind up the nation's wounds." He began to work for a fair peace settlement, which would not be too hard on the South. But on April 14, 1865, five days after General Lee's surrender, Lincoln was shot by a mentally disturbed actor, John Wilkes Booth. He died the next day. Honest Abe was the first U.S. president to be assassinated.

▲ *This portrait shows Lincoln as a young man. It was painted some time after his move, in 1831, from Indiana to Illinois, where he worked as a storekeeper.*

◄ *This famous picture of Lincoln was taken in 1864 by Mathew Brady, one of the first photographers to record the horrors of war. It captures Lincoln's strength and determination as a leader struggling with many difficult decisions.*

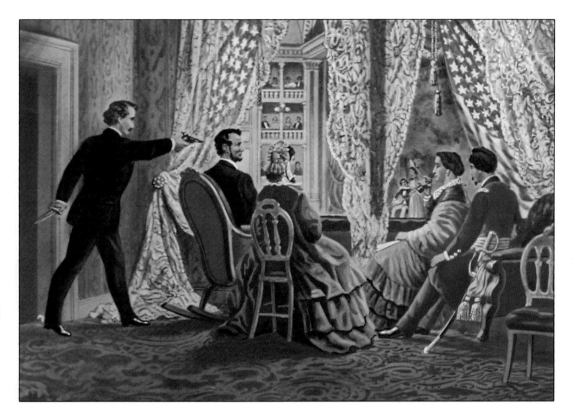

▲ Lincoln with Union officers after the battle of Antietam, September 17, 1862. On "America's bloodiest day," General George McClellan (facing Lincoln) stopped a Confederate advance, but 23,000 were killed or wounded.

▲ Lincoln's assassination as shown by an artist of the time. The president was shot as he watched a play at Ford's Theatre, in Washington, D.C., by a young actor named John Wilkes Booth. Booth escaped but was killed by federal soldiers two weeks later.

◀ Newly freed slaves welcome the victorious Lincoln as he enters Richmond, Virginia, the Confederate capital, on April 4, 1865.

▲ The Lincoln Memorial, in Washington, D.C., was dedicated in 1922. The statue, by Daniel Chester French, is 19 feet tall.

4 Reconstruction and Industry

Andrew Johnson, 17th president, was born in Raleigh, North Carolina, in 1808. With even less education than Abraham Lincoln had, he became a tailor's apprentice at 13, then ran away to begin his own shop. His wife, Eliza, whom he married in 1827, taught him to read and write. Johnson did well as a tailor in Greeneville, Tennessee. He entered local politics as a Democrat and rose to become governor.

As a slaveholder himself, Johnson defended slavery in the Senate. He fought against Lincoln's election in 1860, but when the Civil War broke out, he bravely decided that the Union was more important than Southern rights. He was the only Southern senator to support Lincoln, who appointed him military governor of Tennessee in 1862.

Johnson shared Lincoln's hope for a peace that would bring North and South together again and was chosen as vice president when Lincoln was reelected in 1864. But some Republicans labeled him a rebel sympathizer, and his behavior made matters worse. Weakened by illness, he drank

◀ Johnson came from a poor working family: His father, who died when he was three, was a porter at an inn; his mother, a washerwoman.

▲ In later life, Johnson became the only president to serve as a U.S. senator after being president. He was elected to the Senate in 1875.

whiskey to help him through his inauguration, and the speech he gave was unclear.

Six weeks later, Lincoln was assassinated, and Johnson became president. Republican newspapers called him a drunkard, "touched with insanity." When Congress passed laws to keep ex-Confederates from voting, and limited the president's right to get rid of government officials, Johnson challenged them by firing his secretary of war. He was impeached (charged with official misconduct) by the House of Representatives. The Senate tried him and let him off by a single vote. Although he was not nominated for president in 1868, Tennessee made him their senator in 1875. He died a few months later.

Andrew Johnson (1865–69)

Johnson was impeached, ▶ brought to trial for "high crimes and misdemeanors." The Senate tried him early in 1868, although he was not there in person. He was the only president ever to be impeached, and he won his case by a single vote.

▼ Edwin M. Stanton was secretary of war under both Lincoln and Johnson. After the war, he felt that Johnson was too generous to the South. Johnson fired Stanton, which by law he was not allowed to do. Johnson's enemies brought him to trial in the Senate.

This anti-Johnson cartoon shows ▶ the president as a parrot repeating the word Constitution. Johnson claimed that laws unfair to the defeated South were against the Constitution. His enemies said that he used the Constitution to do favors for the South.

Ulysses S. Grant (1869–77)

Ulysses Simpson Grant, 18th president, was born in Point Pleasant, Ohio, in 1822. He was only an average student at the U.S. Military Academy at West Point. Grant served under General Zachary Taylor in the Mexican War but left the army in 1854, perhaps for a drinking problem. He failed in farming and business, then joined the Union forces at the start of the Civil War.

Grant rose quickly, winning many victories and earning the nickname Unconditional Surrender for his initials. Lincoln made him supreme commander in 1864. In 1865, Grant personally accepted General Robert E. Lee's surrender at Appomattox.

Grant won the presidency for the Republicans as a hero in 1868 and again in 1872. But he was a better general than president. He was conned by cheats and liars, and scandals rocked his administrations. Later, he lost all his savings to a crooked banker. To support his family, he wrote his personal memoirs, even while dying of throat cancer. He finished them four days before he died in 1885. They earned almost half a million dollars.

◀ This portrait shows Grant as he would have wanted to be remembered—as the tough and confident commander in chief of the Union forces.

▼ Cartoonist Thomas Nast makes fun of Northerners who made money off the defeated South and carried their belongings in cheap, carpet-fabric bags.

▲ On April 9, 1865, Grant (at left) accepted the surrender of Confederate commander Robert E. Lee at Appomattox Court House. Grant generously allowed Southern soldiers to keep their personal horses and weapons.

Rutherford B. Hayes (1877–81)

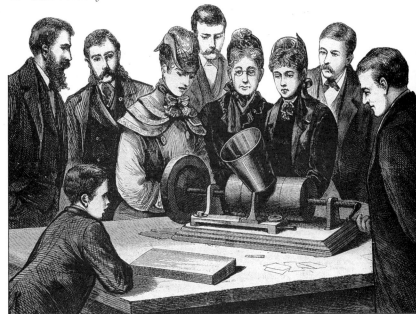

Samuel J. Tilden, governor of New York. In the presidential election of 1876, more people voted for Tilden than for Hayes. But after arguments over the vote count, Tilden lost. Hayes was criticized for his "stolen victory."

In 1877, President Hayes asked the brilliant young inventor Thomas Alva Edison to demonstrate this amazing "phonograph" in the White House. The machine, worked by a crank, recorded and played back voices and sounds.

Grant (standing in front of tree) with a group of his officers during the Civil War. Grant was grim and firm as a soldier. Some felt he did what he had to; others called him a butcher.

When Hayes withdrew all federal troops from Southern states and returned their powers to them, he did not guarantee civil rights for black Americans.

Rutherford Birchard Hayes, 19th president, was born in Delaware, Ohio, in 1822. He went to Kenyon College and Harvard Law School. As a lawyer, he defended runaway slaves.

Hayes rose to the rank of major general in the Civil War. In 1876, as a Union war hero with a clean political record, he became the Republican candidate for president. He lost the election to Democrat Samuel J. Tilden, but people argued that the votes had not been counted correctly, and Congress gave Hayes the presidency. Some disagreed and nicknamed him Rutherfraud.

As president, Hayes put down riots by striking railroad workers and tried to make government workers more honest. In 1877, he officially withdrew all remaining federal troops from the South, ending the era called Reconstruction, in which the defeated states had been badly treated. Hayes's wife banned drinking, smoking, and dancing in the White House, and began the custom of Easter-egg rolling on the lawn. Hayes had promised to serve only one term. He worked for charities until his death in 1893.

James Garfield (1881)

James Abram Garfield, 20th president, was born near Orange, Ohio, in 1831. He was the last president born in a log cabin. Garfield became a classics professor—he amazed people by writing Latin with one hand and Greek with the other, at the same time. He was also a lawyer and, at 30, was at one time the youngest Union general in the Civil War.

Garfield served for 17 years in Congress and became the Republican candidate for the presidency in 1880, narrowly winning the popular vote. When many Republicans begged for White House jobs, he exclaimed, "My God! What is there in this place that a man should ever want to get in it?" On July 2, 1881, after four months in office, Garfield was shot by the mentally disturbed Charles J. Guiteau, who had been refused work as a diplomat. It took Garfield 80 days to die.

▼ Garfield's imposing looks and friendly manner made him popular, but he did little to stop government corruption.

▲ Shiloh, where Garfield fought in April 1862. There were more than 10,000 losses on each side. In 1863, he was promoted to major general for his bravery at Chickamauga.

▼ Secretary of State James G. Blaine (right) watches in horror as Garfield is gunned down at the Washington railroad station by mentally disturbed Charles J. Guiteau.

Chester A. Arthur (1881–85)

Chester Alan Arthur, 21st president, was born in Fairfield, Vermont, in 1829. A lawyer, noted for civil rights work on behalf of black Americans, he was a top Union staff officer in the Civil War.

Having worked hard for the Republican party, in 1871, Arthur was appointed by President Grant to the powerful post of collector of the port of New York. Seven years later, President Hayes fired him, charging that he had used tax money to reward supporters. Many believed he had been unfairly treated and made him Arthur Garfield's vice president. On Garfield's death in 1881, Arthur became the third president in a single year. Political corruption did not flourish under the luxury-loving "gentleman boss." Arthur was efficient and upright, and worked to reform the civil service. He did not run in 1884, for he knew he had kidney disease.

He died two years later.

▲ *A contemporary cartoon shows Arthur's supporter, Republican Senator Roscoe Conkling, manipulating the New York political "machine."*

"Elegant Arthur" ▶ *was known to like fine clothes and high society. He nevertheless proved a competent, honest, and dignified president.*

▲ *Arthur's term saw the opening of the Brooklyn Bridge and the building, in Chicago, of the first skyscraper.*

Grover Cleveland (1885–89), (1893–97)

Grover Cleveland, 22nd and 24th president, was born in Caldwell, New Jersey, in 1837. He was the only president to serve two terms that did not follow each other. He became a tough, honest mayor of Buffalo and governor of New York.

In 1884, Cleveland was elected the first Democratic president in 28 years as an upright man, hard on corruption. His drive for lower taxes on imports annoyed big business. On his defeat in 1888, he declared there was "no happier man in the United States," but he ran again and was reelected four years later. This time, he disappointed businessmen by failing to improve the economy and angered workers by using federal troops against strikers. After a secret operation in his second term, he did not try for a third.

Cleveland was the only president to be married in the White House, and his daughter Esther was the only president's child born there. On his deathbed in 1908, he said, "I have tried so hard to do right."

▲ Cleveland's marriage to his former ward, 21-year-old Frances Folsom, at the White House, in June 1886, made her the youngest first lady ever. Cleveland himself was 49.

▲ Grover Cleveland used his presidential veto to override the wishes of Congress over 300 times, more than twice as often as all the earlier presidents together had.

Cleveland was plump, good-humored, and hated corruption. ▶ Some called him Grover the Good. He wrote Presidential Problems, a book explaining his stand on major issues.

Benjamin Harrison (1889–93)

Benjamin Harrison, 23rd president, was born in North Bend, Ohio, in 1833. He was the grandson of President William Henry Harrison. Harrison became a successful lawyer and U.S. senator from Indiana, but his Civil War record as a commander of Union infantry got him the Republican nomination in 1888. "Grandfather's hat fits Ben," sang his supporters, and he won over Grover Cleveland, who had not fought in the war.

Although Harrison signed into law the Sherman Antitrust Act, curbing the power of big business, many thought he favored the rich, and he was called Kid Gloves Harrison. Votes taken from the Republicans by the new Populist party, supported mainly by farmers and workers, contributed to his defeat in 1892, when Cleveland won a second term. Before Harrison died in 1901, he called the White House "my jail."

▲ A cartoon view of the mugwumps, Republicans who supported Democrat Cleveland in the 1884 presidential campaign. They considered the Republican candidate, James G. Blaine, a corrupt "machine" politician.

▲ Benjamin Harrison is sworn in as president, on March 4, 1889. In 1891, electricity was installed in the White House. After getting a shock, Harrison refused to touch a switch and often went to bed with the lights on.

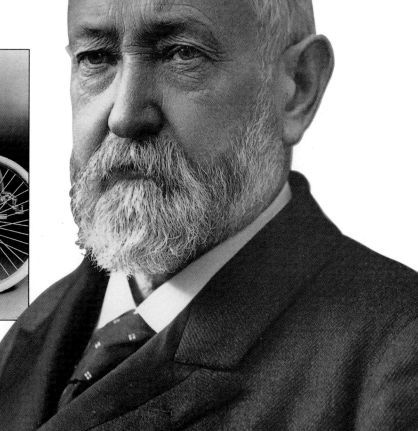

▲ In 1896, during Cleveland's second term, Henry Ford brought out the first automobile in Detroit. This quadricycle was a forerunner of the famous Model T of 1908.

President Harrison was ▶ able and hardworking but lacked personal charm. He was once described as "a marble statue." During his term, six new states joined the Union.

William McKinley (1897–1901)

William McKinley, 25th president, was born in Niles, Ohio, in 1843, the seventh child of a wealthy businessman. He enlisted in a Union regiment commanded by future President Hayes and was promoted to lieutenant for bravery in action. McKinley was the last president to have fought in the Civil War.

A lawyer, as were 25 of the 40 men who became president, McKinley entered Ohio politics as a Republican in 1869. In Congress, he supported high taxes on imports to protect American industry, and his presidential bid in 1896 was masterminded by the millionaire businessman Marcus Hanna. The Democratic candidate, William Jennings Bryan, noisily attacked the "rule of the rich." But McKinley ran a calm "front porch" campaign from Canton, Ohio, refusing to leave his invalid wife, and still won a convincing victory.

Some feared McKinley would be a puppet of big business. But although tariffs rose to record heights and business boomed, his administration also laid the foundation for America's 20th-century role as a world power. He hesitated to involve America in Cuba's struggle for independence from Spain, but when the Spanish-American War could no longer be avoided, he was a confident and successful leader. As a result, in 1898, the Philippines and Puerto Rico became U.S. possessions. McKinley also annexed Hawaii and opened up trade with China.

General prosperity won McKinley a second victory over Bryan in 1900. His campaign slogan was "Four years more of the full dinner pail." McKinley planned to reduce tariffs in order to encourage international trade. But on September 6, 1901, he was shot by anarchist Leon Czolgosz. As his bodyguards tackled the gunman, the wounded president cried, "Don't hurt him, boys!" He died eight days later.

◀ *This formal portrait shows McKinley as stern and serious. In reality, he was generous and kind, devoted to his invalid wife, who suffered from a seizure disorder.*

William Jennings Bryan, three ▶ *times defeated for the presidency, makes one of the rousing speeches that won him fame.*

The "full dinner pail" stood ▲ for prosperity under McKinley and helped him win a second term in 1900.

Leon Czolgosz, his gun ▼ hidden under a handkerchief, fatally shoots McKinley at the Pan-American Exposition in Buffalo. He was electrocuted less than three months later.

▲ On February 16, 1898, the battleship USS Maine *blew up at Havana, Cuba. Although there was no proof Spanish agents were responsible, war was declared two months later.*

▲ McKinley tried to avoid war with Spain and was unfairly attacked as a coward. His vice president, Theodore Roosevelt, privately called him "a white-livered cur."

5 World Conflict and a New Century

Theodore Roosevelt, 26th president, was born to a wealthy family in New York City in 1858. He was a sickly child but vowed to live a "strenuous life." He took up riding, swimming, and boxing, and, after studying at Harvard and entering Republican politics in New York, spent two years on a cattle ranch. He was a man of boundless energy, a historian, naturalist, and hunter. As president, he created more than a million acres of national forests and parks. The original teddy bear got its name from a baby bear Roosevelt found in the wilderness.

In 1898, at the beginning of the Spanish-American War, Roosevelt resigned as assistant secretary of the navy to put together a cavalry regiment. In Cuba, he led his Rough Riders in a celebrated charge up San Juan Hill. The following year, he became governor of New York.

Roosevelt was chosen as vice president in 1900. In September 1901, McKinley died, and Roosevelt became, at 42, the youngest of all the presidents. As president, he worked to keep big businesses from joining together to damage smaller ones and was labeled a "damned cowboy." But his "square deal" reforms generally improved lives without hurting business. In foreign affairs, his motto was "Speak softly and carry a big stick," a mixture of diplomacy and toughness that strengthened America as a world power and ensured U.S. control over the new Panama Canal between the Atlantic and Pacific oceans. Roosevelt was easily reelected in 1904. In 1906, he became the first American to win the Nobel Peace Prize, for his part in settling the Russo-Japanese War.

Roosevelt did not seek reelection in 1908. In 1912, he stood as a Progressive (Bull Moose) party candidate, taking Republican votes and giving the Democrat, Woodrow Wilson, an easy victory. In his last years, he explored a river in Brazil, which was named the Rio Teodoro in his honor. After 1914, Roosevelt pushed for America's entry into the First World War. His son Quentin would be killed in an air battle over France. He himself died of a heart attack in January 1919. He said, "No president has ever enjoyed himself as much as I have."

◀ Roosevelt at the age of 26, in hunting gear. Although very nearsighted, he preferred to be seen without glasses. In later life, a boxing accident left him blind in one eye.

Theodore Roosevelt (1901–9)

◀ Colonel Roosevelt stands beneath the flag at the head of his Rough Riders, just after the battle on San Juan Hill. He called it "the greatest day of my life."

▲ Roosevelt meets with Russian and Japanese diplomats at Portsmouth, New Hampshire, to help negotiate an end to the Russo-Japanese War.

▲ Hunting trophies dominate the North Room at Sagamore Hill, Roosevelt's home on New York's Long Island. It is now a national historic site.

Looking every inch the world statesman, President Roosevelt posed for this fine portrait by John Singer Sargent in 1903. ▶

William H. Taft (1909–13)

William Howard Taft, 27th president, was born in Cincinnati, Ohio, in 1857. He was the son of a judge and Republican politician who became President Grant's secretary of war.

Educated at Yale, Taft won a fine reputation in Ohio as a lawyer and in 1890 became U.S. solicitor general. From 1901 to 1904, he served kindly and fairly as governor of the Philippines, which had just become a U.S. territory in the Spanish-American War, expertly managing the change from military to civilian rule. Made secretary of war in 1904, Taft became a close friend of President Theodore Roosevelt, who made sure that Taft got the Republican nomination in 1908. He easily beat Democrat William Jennings Bryan, who was running for the third and last time.

Taft was the largest man to be president, his six-foot-two-inch frame weighing more than 300 pounds. But his personality did not match his size, and he seemed dull and overcautious after the colorful Roosevelt. Reluctant to make decisions, Taft annoyed both conservative and progressive Republicans, and was accused of failing to carry through important land conservation measures Roosevelt had introduced. In the 1912 election, Roosevelt ran as an independent, taking votes away from his old friend. Wilson, the Democrat, won by a huge majority.

Taft said he was glad to leave the White House, "the lonesomest place in the world," and was far more comfortable teaching constitutional law at Yale. In 1921, he became chief justice of the U.S. Supreme Court, a job he greatly enjoyed. As the only ex-president ever to occupy this post, he swore Presidents Coolidge and Hoover into office. He stepped down because of illness in 1930 and died the same year. His son, Senator Robert Taft, would fiercely oppose President Franklin D. Roosevelt and unsuccessfully try for the Republican nomination himself in 1940, 1948, and 1952.

Taft greets a Filipino leader ▶ during his term as governor of the Philippines (1901–4). His enlightened rule laid the foundations of self-government for the islands.

▼ The massive, mild-mannered Taft was once described as looking like "a gentle and kind American bison." In politics, he was a conservative at a time when many were becoming more radical.

▲ In 1910, President Taft began a tradition by tossing out the first ball of the major league baseball season. His own favorite sports were golf, tennis, and horseback riding.

▲ Early moviemakers create an Egyptian village in California. When Taft was president, the movie industry grew rapidly. The first motion picture studio was set up in 1911 in Hollywood.

A seated portrait of the ▶ impressive Taft. It is said that extra-large chairs and an outsize bathtub were bought for him at the White House.

Woodrow Wilson (1913–21)

Woodrow Wilson, 28th president, was born in Staunton, Virginia, in 1856. He taught law and politics, becoming a professor at Princeton University in 1890 and, 12 years later, its president.

At Princeton, Wilson greatly improved teaching methods, but in 1910, when his plans for more reforms were rejected, he resigned to become a "schoolmaster in politics." He was elected governor of New Jersey and reformed the state government so well that he won the Democratic presidential nomination in 1912. He won an easy victory over the Republicans.

Wilson's New Freedom program resulted in lower taxes on goods brought into the country, an improved banking system, and better conditions for workers. He was the first president to hold regular press conferences to explain his policies, and he also spoke on the radio.

In 1916, Wilson sent troops into Mexico without hesitation against the revolutionary Pancho Villa. But the same year, he did his best to keep America out of World War I. He narrowly won reelection with the slogan "He kept us [U.S.] out of war." But German submarines attacked American ships, and on April 6, 1917, Congress did declare war. Wilson promised "to make the world safe for democracy."

On January 8, 1918, Wilson issued his Fourteen Points, a plan for a lasting peace and international brotherhood through a League of Nations. At the Paris Peace Conference in 1919, he persuaded world leaders to include most of his proposals into the Versailles Treaty. But the U.S. Senate refused to accept the treaty, keeping America out of the League of Nations.

It was a crushing blow for Wilson. In September 1919, he collapsed during a grueling campaign to raise support for the league, and suffered a stroke. Afterward, he was too ill to take part in government. In the 1920 election, the Republicans won an overwhelming victory, but Wilson was awarded the Nobel Peace Prize that December. In 1924, he died in his sleep.

Wilson entered politics not for personal gain, but to do what he thought best for his country. He had had trouble learning to read but became the most highly educated president. ▶

◀ (upper left) *On May 7, 1915, 128 American lives were lost when the British liner* Lusitania *was torpedoed by a German submarine. Many Americans called for war.*

▲ *On April 2, 1917, Wilson asks a joint session of Congress for a declaration of war on Germany. War was declared four days later.*

A steel-helmeted doughboy, ▲ *as U.S. soldiers were called in World War I. By mid-1918, there were more than 1.5 million American troops in France.*

President Wilson, British Prime ▶ *Minister David Lloyd George (left),* and French Premier Georges Clemenceau appear together at the Paris Peace Conference, 1919. Wilson was the first president to visit Europe.*

Warren G. Harding (1921–23)

Warren Gamaliel Harding, 29th president, was born near what is now Blooming Grove, Ohio, in 1865. As a newspaper owner, Harding published editorials favoring business concerns. By 1914, he was a U.S. senator.

Harding was easy to get along with, spoke well, and "looked like a president"; he gained the Republican nomination in 1920. The 19th amendment to the Constitution, giving American women the right to vote, was passed the same year, and Harding's good looks were expected to bring support from female voters. He also promised a "return to normalcy" after the First World War and won by a landslide. Harding promised to choose the "best minds" to advise him, and he did appoint some good men. But his administration became known for its corruption. Harding died suddenly in 1923, missing the Teapot Dome scandal, which ruined important men he himself had chosen.

A government agent takes an ax to barrels of beer. From 1919 to 1933, the era of Prohibition, the making and selling of alcoholic drinks was illegal.

Cartoonists had a field day when an oil field scandal in the Teapot Dome area of Wyoming revealed corruption in Harding's administration.

◄ Warren Harding was elected on the slogan "Back to normalcy," promising peace and prosperity after the war years. Handsome, dignified, and a fine speaker, he seemed well suited to high office.

▲ Delegates pack the Republican National Convention in Chicago, 1920. Harding's nomination is said to have been decided upon at a meeting of party leaders in "a smoke-filled room."

Calvin Coolidge (1923–29)

Calvin Coolidge, here ▲ operating a hayfork, was said to share the virtues of the early American pioneers.

Dancers demonstrate the ▼ Charleston, one of the crazes of the Jazz Age. Many Americans in the Roaring Twenties did not share Coolidge's devotion to the quiet life.

Calvin Coolidge, 30th president, was born in Plymouth, Vermont, in 1872. He attracted national attention in 1919 when, as governor of Massachusetts, he used state troops to crush a strike by Boston policemen. The respectable Coolidge was the Republican vice presidential choice in 1920 and came into office on President Harding's death in August 1923. After firing dishonest officials appointed by Harding, he easily won the 1924 election.

Coolidge believed that "the business of America is business." The stock market boomed, but farmers, miners, and veterans suffered. Coolidge's policies eventually led to a major economic crisis but seemed a great success at the end of his term. He surprised everyone by announcing he would not seek reelection in 1928, saying simply, "I do not choose to run for president." He died in 1933.

◄ Coolidge was a tightwad. His election slogan was "Keep cool with Coolidge," and he served ice water to White House visitors.

Herbert Hoover (1929–33)

Herbert Clark Hoover, 31st president, was born in West Branch, Iowa, in 1874. He was orphaned at 8 and raised by Quaker relatives. Hoover became a world-famous mining engineer and, by the age of 40, a millionaire.

In 1914, when World War I began, Hoover volunteered to head a group fighting hunger in war-torn Europe, and helped bring stranded Americans home. He continued with his relief efforts when America entered the war in 1917, overseeing food supply all over Europe, from Belgium to the Soviet Union. His hard work was responsible for saving thousands of lives.

Hoover became so well respected that both parties thought of him as a possible presidential candidate in 1920. Declaring himself a Republican, he was named secretary of commerce under Harding and Coolidge. When Coolidge refused to run again in 1928, Hoover was easily elected, promising "a chicken in every pot." But in October 1929, the U.S. stock market collapsed, followed by the economic disaster of the Great Depression, which lasted until 1934. Hoover was blamed for the crisis, which threw millions out of work.

Hoover believed that government should stay out of people's lives, and trusted that the know-how and effort of ordinary Americans would somehow make things better. He did little to relieve hardship. The country was plunged into despair, and people who had lost everything lived in miserable shantytowns, which they called Hoovervilles. In 1932, he was overwhelmingly defeated by Democrat Franklin D. Roosevelt.

In World War II, Hoover returned to famine relief and later headed groups studying government reorganization, which made important suggestions for reform. He gave all his earnings from this work to charity. He died in 1964 at the age of 90, better remembered as a humanitarian than as an unsuccessful president.

◀ Herbert Hoover was a genius at organization but failed to solve America's economic problems.

The elderly Hoover is honored ▶ in 1947 for his lifelong work with charities. Colorado's Boulder Dam was renamed for him.

People who lost all their money when the stock market failed tried to sell their possessions for cash to feed their families.

▼ In 1932, a "bonus army" of jobless veterans marched on Washington, demanding payment of bonuses promised for war service.

▲ Worried crowds fill the sidewalk outside the New York Stock Exchange at the time of the October 1929 Wall Street crash. Some killed themselves when they were ruined.

Police clash with "bonus ▶ marchers" who set up camp in the nation's capital. Federal troops scattered 9,000.

Franklin D. Roosevelt (1933–45)

Franklin Delano Roosevelt, 32nd president, was born on his family's estate in Hyde Park, New York, in 1882. He was a distant cousin of Theodore Roosevelt, whose niece, Eleanor, he married in 1905. He entered Democratic politics as a New York state senator in 1910 and was assistant secretary of the navy until 1920. In 1921, he was crippled by polio but continued his career through sheer will and years of painful exercise. He would never walk again without help.

Elected governor of New York in 1928, Roosevelt pioneered unemployment relief during the Great Depression, winning the Democratic nomination and a landslide victory in 1932. He began his term by calling a special session of Congress, the Hundred Days, to approve his plan for a New Deal. This great program for relief and recovery helped farmers and workers, setting up government agencies and projects to make jobs for millions of unemployed. Some Americans were worried by increases in federal government controls and the president's own powers, but Roosevelt's successes, and his "fireside chats" over the radio, brought confidence back to a despairing people. He gained another huge victory in the 1936 election and won again in 1940 and 1944. He was the only president to serve more than two terms.

When World War II began in 1939, Roosevelt promised Great Britain "all aid short of war." In December 1941, Japanese forces attacked the U.S. fleet at Pearl Harbor in the Pacific, and America joined forces with the Allies, primarily Great Britain and Russia, against the Axis powers, Germany and Japan.

Roosevelt traveled back and forth to oversee strategy and keep the Allied nations working together. With victory assured, he planned a postwar peace with other Allied leaders but died suddenly on April 12, 1945, just days before the war's end. He had been president for more than 12 years.

◀ Roosevelt delights in his reelection, by a tremendous majority, as governor of New York in November 1930.

Through a mass of ▶ microphones, the president broadcasts one of his "fireside chats" to the nation.

◀ A 1945 portrait of Roosevelt with his characteristic cigarette holder. Artist Douglas Chandor was fascinated by the president's expressive hands.

▲ Eleanor Roosevelt finds time to chat at ceremonies marking the beginning of a slum clearance program in Detroit, 1930. The first lady's untiring work to help disadvantaged Americans continued long after her husband's death.

Roosevelt meets with British ▶ Prime Minister Winston Churchill (left) and Soviet leader Joseph Stalin at the Yalta Conference, February 1945. They discussed the final steps for defeating Germany and Japan, and helped shape the postwar world.

Modern America   *Harry S Truman (1945–53)*

Harry S Truman, 33rd president, was born in Lamar, Missouri, in 1884. He worked as a farmer and served in France as an artillery officer in World War I. After failing in business, he entered politics. Elected as a Democratic U.S. senator in 1935, Truman strongly supported Roosevelt's New Deal. He worked to combat waste in military spending during World War II, becoming vice president in 1945. When Roosevelt died only 83 days into his fourth term, Truman became president and made gains in civil rights. In 1948, the plainspoken "Give-'em-Hell, Harry" narrowly won reelection.

Truman's motto was "If you can't stand the heat, get out of the kitchen!" He proved his own ability to accept great responsibility by deciding to use the atomic bomb against Japan. Many thousands of people died in the total destruction of Hiroshima and Nagasaki on August 6 and 9, 1945, saving the lives of many thousands of Allied servicemen when Japan surrendered a few days later.

When World War II ended, the cold war, with tension but no head-on conflict, began between the West and the major Communist powers. Truman took a tough line, promising U.S. money and military aid to all "free peoples" menaced by communism. In 1949, he played a leading part in setting up the Western military alliance known as NATO (the North Atlantic Treaty Organization) and committed U.S. troops to fight against communism in the Korean War.

At home, Truman was frustrated. His Fair Deal policies for social reform were blocked by Congress. When he stood against sweeping "anti-Red" laws, he was accused of being "soft on communism." He fired Douglas MacArthur, his chief commander in Korea, for going against his military decisions, and the Korean War dragged on. In 1952, Truman did not seek reelection. He died 20 years later, asking these simple words in his memory: "He did his damndest."

◀ *Competence and common sense* ▶ *were the hallmarks of straight-talking Harry Truman, who took on great responsibilities without complaint. A sign on his desk read* THE BUCK STOPS HERE.

(far left) *In April 1945, new President Truman sits for the camera with his wife, Bess (whom he called the Boss), and daughter, Margaret, perched beside him. When people criticized Margaret's performances as a concert singer, the president was furious.*

In April 1945, representatives of 60 nations met in San Francisco to draw up the charter of the United Nations. Here, Truman addresses the final session of the conference. On August 8, he signed the charter, confirming the United States' membership.

Immediately after his reelection in 1948, President Truman and his family leave their hometown, Independence, Missouri, to return to Washington, D.C.

General Douglas MacArthur, commander of U.S. forces in the Korean War, challenged Truman's military judgment and was fired.

Dwight D. Eisenhower (1953–61)

Dwight David Eisenhower, 34th president, was born in Denison, Texas, in 1890. He graduated from the military academy at West Point in 1915 and became a career soldier. In World War II, he was appointed supreme Allied commander for the invasion of Europe. A friendly man who could also be tough, he used patience and tact to keep Allied commanders working together smoothly under his leadership.

The Allied victory in 1945 made Eisenhower a hero, and in 1952, he was approached as a presidential candidate by both parties. He chose the Republicans and won by a large margin over Democrat Adlai Stevenson, with the slogan "I like Ike." He scored another major victory in 1956.

Eisenhower worked for world peace. In 1953, he ended the Korean War and, in 1956, forced Britain, France, and Israel to let the United Nations oversee Egyptian control of the Suez Canal linking the Red Sea and the Mediterranean. In 1955, he suggested arms limitation measures to Soviet leaders. But he felt America had to stand firm in the cold war. To control Communist spread in the Middle East, he sent U.S. troops to Lebanon in 1958. His secretary of state, John Foster Dulles, threatened to use nuclear weapons against any Soviet aggression.

At home, Eisenhower improved social welfare programs and moved ahead on civil rights for all Americans. In 1957, he sent troops to watch over the integration of black and white schools in Little Rock, Arkansas. He also resisted extreme "anti-Red" laws demanded by Communist-hating Senator Joseph McCarthy and his supporters. In 1951, the 22nd Amendment to the Constitution limited U.S. presidents to two elected terms. Eisenhower, in poor health, would not have run again in 1960, anyway. He advised later presidents until his death in 1969.

▲ Eisenhower was one of the finest soldiers the United States has ever seen. He began World War II as a lieutenant colonel. By December 1944, he had reached the five-star rank of General of the Army.

In 1959, Soviet Premier Nikita ▶ Khrushchev, shading his eyes with his hat, is welcomed by President Eisenhower at Andrews Air Force Base in Maryland. He was the first Russian Communist leader to visit the United States.

◀ Eisenhower, seen here in 1960, loved to play golf. He was criticized for relaxing on the golf course at times of international tension.

◀ *This wartime meeting in December 1944 between supreme Allied Commander Eisenhower and British supreme Field Marshal Montgomery looks friendly, but the two great leaders often disagreed on strategy.*

▼ *Fidel Castro established himself as Communist dictator of Cuba in 1959. Two years later, he seized property belonging to U.S. companies on the island, and President Eisenhower broke off diplomatic relations.*

John F. Kennedy (1961–63)

John Fitzgerald Kennedy, 35th president, was born in Brookline, Massachusetts, in 1917. He was the second son of millionaire businessman Joseph P. Kennedy, who was determined to make one of his children president. When the eldest son died in action in World War II, the family's power and influence were put behind John.

John Kennedy, known as Jack, was decorated for bravery as a patrol boat commander. The handsome war hero was elected a Democratic congressman in 1946 and a U.S. senator in 1952. A long, well-organized campaign won him the presidential nomination in 1960. He bested Republican candidate Richard Nixon in a series of televised debates and won a narrow victory. At 43, he was the youngest president ever elected (Theodore Roosevelt took over at 42 from McKinley) and the first Roman Catholic to take office.

Under Jack Kennedy and his wife, Jackie, the White House seemed a new Camelot, the focus of American hopes and ideals. Kennedy was especially popular with young people, and many volunteered to help underdeveloped countries in his Peace Corps program. He increased spending for defense and vowed to put a man on the moon. But the advance of the New Frontier, Kennedy's plan for improved civil rights, education, and medical care, was blocked by Congress.

Kennedy approved the disastrous Bay of Pigs invasion of Cuba in 1961 and stepped up military aid to South Vietnam. In 1962, he went to the edge of war, blocking Havana harbor until the Soviets removed nuclear missiles from Cuban bases. Soviets agreed to a nuclear test-ban treaty the following year.

On November 22, 1963, Kennedy was fatally shot as he rode in an open car in Dallas, Texas. The gunman, Lee Harvey Oswald, was himself murdered two days later. An investigation concluded that Oswald had acted alone, but questions remained, and many felt he had been part of a larger conspiracy. In 1968, Kennedy's younger brother Robert was assassinated while campaigning for the Democratic nomination.

▲ *The Kennedy family in 1934. Joseph, Sr., holds baby Edward. Jack sits at the left, and brother Robert stands behind his father.*

▼ *A relaxed President Kennedy sits for an informal portrait in the rocking chair that was his favorite seat in the White House.*

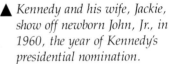

▲ Kennedy and his wife, Jackie, show off newborn John, Jr., in 1960, the year of Kennedy's presidential nomination.

◄ Visiting Europe in 1963, Kennedy looks over the Berlin Wall that divided West Berlin from Communist East Berlin. The wall was torn down in 1989, and the city reunited.

The Kennedys mourn. ► John, Jr., on his third birthday, bravely salutes his father's casket, as Kennedy is carried to his final resting place in Arlington National Cemetery.

▼ Singer Frank Sinatra with Senator Kennedy in 1960. Many show business personalities supported Kennedy's successful presidential campaign.

Lyndon B. Johnson (1963–69)

Lyndon Baines Johnson, 36th president, was a farmer's son, born near Stonewall, Texas, in 1908. A schoolteacher and local politician, he was elected a U.S. congressman in 1937 and became a firm supporter of Roosevelt's New Deal. In 1948, he was elected to the Senate, where his skill as a wheeler-dealer, bargaining and smoothing out arguments, made him Democratic majority leader in 1955. He lost the presidential nomination to Kennedy in 1960 but, as a conservative southern Protestant, made an ideal running mate for the liberal, northern Roman Catholic. In 1963, Kennedy's assassination made Johnson president.

Johnson's Great Society program put Kennedy's civil rights and social welfare ideas into action, including his "war on poverty." In the 1964 election, Johnson won a record share of the popular vote against Barry Goldwater, who called for much stronger military action against communism. But Johnson himself soon asked Congress for greater powers in the Vietnam conflict. Granted use of "all necessary measures," he ordered the bombing of North Vietnam and began a massive increase in the number of U.S.

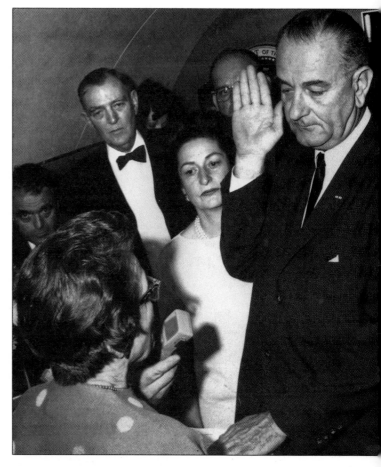

◀ Lyndon Johnson was the first Texan in the White House. In the Texas tradition, he was tough, shrewd, and hearty.

▲ Within two hours of Kennedy's death, Johnson was sworn into office aboard the presidential airplane.

troops in Vietnam, which reached half a million by 1968. Although some Americans went "all the way with LBJ," many took to the streets to protest the war. Race riots also divided American society.

Johnson's unpopularity reached its height early in 1968, when the Communist Tet Offensive in Vietnam contradicted his claims that victory was near. He stopped the bombing of North Vietnam and promised that the United States would seek a peaceful solution. Tired, ill, and heartbroken by such slogans as "Hey, hey, LBJ: How many kids did you kill today?" he announced that he would not seek reelection, and retired to his Texas ranch until his death on January 2, 1973. A peace agreement was signed in Paris the next day, and the war was over.

▲ Johnson with one of his dogs. Animal lovers objected to his habit of making his beagle bark by pulling its ears. The president liked the image of himself as a down-home country boy and was often photographed with animals, on horseback, or herding cattle.

◄ Many thousands of demonstrators gather outside the Pentagon, October 1967, to protest America's role in the Vietnam War. One banner labels Johnson a war criminal. Much savage criticism was directed at the president personally.

Richard M. Nixon (1969–74)

Richard Milhous Nixon, 37th president, was born in Yorba Linda, California, in 1913. Trained as a lawyer, he was elected a Republican congressman in 1947 and a senator in 1950. A tough stand against communism, and political skill so ruthless it earned him the nickname Tricky Dick, won Nixon the vice presidency under Eisenhower. Nominated for president in 1960, he was narrowly defeated by Kennedy. But in 1968, when the Democrats were being blamed for the Vietnam War, he won by a small majority.

Nixon promised "peace with honor" in Vietnam. As president, he began to withdraw U.S. troops but tried to force the North Vietnamese to the peace table by sending more planes against them, bombing Communist bases in Cambodia and moving troops into Cambodia and Laos. Early in 1973, Communist leaders agreed to a truce and all U.S. troops were withdrawn. The next year, fighting began again, but Congress refused to increase military aid. South Vietnam fell to the Communists in April 1975.

Elsewhere, Nixon did better in foreign affairs, taking great strides in relations with Communist China and the Soviet Union. In 1972, he made a historic visit to Peking and in Moscow signed an agreement to limit nuclear arms.

The Nixon years also saw improvement in the economy at home and the first human to set foot on the moon. Announcing "peace is at hand," Nixon won a landslide victory in 1972. But his triumph was short-lived. In 1973, Vice President Spiro Agnew resigned, charged with bribery. Soon after, Nixon and his aides were accused of encouraging the burglary of Democratic party headquarters in the Watergate office complex during Nixon's reelection campaign. Nixon had denied knowing anything about the incident, and he continued his cover-up, refusing to produce important evidence. In July 1974, Congress voted for his impeachment. The next month, before he could be questioned, Nixon became the only president ever to resign. He had undermined the respect and trust Americans felt for the office of president.

▲ Nixon, seated at right, takes part in a 1947 hearing of the House Un-American Activities Committee (HUAC), which investigated communism in the United States. Nixon's activities on the committee first brought him attention in Congress.

▼ Vice President Nixon and Senator John Kennedy shake hands after a television debate in the 1960 election campaign. Kennedy did better in these debates, which helped him win a narrow victory.

▲ This flattering portrait is by the famous American illustrator Norman Rockwell. Nixon photographed badly, and people asked, "Would you buy a used car from this man?"

▲ Nixon and Chinese Premier Chou En-lai inspect an honor guard as the president arrives in Communist China in 1972. Nixon was the first president to visit either China or Soviet Russia.

"Some of my judgments ▶ were wrong" was the only apology Nixon made when he resigned in disgrace in 1974.

Gerald R. Ford, Jr. (1974–77)

Gerald Rudolph Ford, Jr., 38th president, was born in 1913 in Omaha, Nebraska. He began life as Leslie Kynch King, Jr.; his name was changed by adoption. A football star in college, Ford became a lawyer and served as a solid and reliable Republican congressman for 25 years. In 1973, he was chosen by Nixon to replace the disgraced Vice President Agnew.

On August 9, 1974, Nixon resigned, and Ford became president. He was the only man to be both vice president and president without winning election to either office. Ford pardoned Nixon for any federal crimes he might have committed on the job. This widely unpopular move was balanced in 1975 by his prompt action in flying many thousands of refugees out of South Vietnam, and in sending U.S. Marines to free the American freighter *Mayaguez* from Cambodian Communists. He was nominated for president in 1976 but lost by a close margin.

▼ *Triumphant Communist troops enter the capital of South Vietnam in April 1975. Congress had refused Ford's request for emergency military aid to South Vietnam.*

Although he was criticized for ▶ pardoning former President Nixon, Gerald Ford's straightforwardness and honesty helped to restore confidence in government.

A solemn-faced Gerald Ford, unexpectedly raised to the presidency, takes the oath of

office from Chief Justice ▶ Warren Burger, on August 9, 1974.

James Earl Carter, Jr. (1977–81)

James Earl Carter, Jr., 39th president, was born in Plains, Georgia, in 1924. A graduate of the U.S. Naval Academy at Annapolis, he served as a naval officer but resigned to run his family's peanut farm. Elected governor of Georgia in 1970, he was praised for his civil rights program and in 1976 won the presidency as a Democrat.

With no experience in national politics, Jimmy Carter had a hard time getting Congress to carry out his policies. He had trouble with economic problems, caused partly by the world oil shortage. And in 1980, a military mission to rescue American hostages from Iran failed miserably. In 1978, Carter organized talks at Camp David between Israel and Egypt, resulting in a peace treaty. But the following year, relations with the Soviet Union were strained when Russia invaded Afghanistan. Carter lost the 1980 election by a record margin and retired from politics to do charity work.

▼ Carter with Egypt's President Anwar el-Sadat. Carter arranged a major treaty between Egypt and Israel.

Carter lost reelection▼ but was a dedicated president, dealing with forces beyond his control.

The Ayatollah Khomeini's ▲ religious dictatorship and hatred for America meant trouble. Khomeini seized power in Iran in 1979 and took American hostages.

Ronald Reagan (1981–89)

Ronald Wilson Reagan, 40th president, was born in Tampico, Illinois, in 1911. A college athlete, he became a radio sports reporter, then in 1937 went to Hollywood and appeared in over 50 movies. While president of the Screen Actors Guild, Reagan was a Democrat, but in 1964, he loudly supported right-wing Republican presidential candidate Barry Goldwater. Governor of California from 1967 to 1974, he won the Republican presidential nomination in 1980 on the third try. His sweeping victory at 69 made him the oldest man ever elected president.

Reagan aimed to boost the economy by cutting taxes to encourage business, but Reaganomics seemed to favor big corporations at the expense of welfare, conservation, and the "little guy." The economy was marked by short-lived booms and heavy slumps, and many were out of work. Reagan stood firm against what he viewed as the "evil empire" of communism, and spent a lot of money on defense. His ambitious program for a missile system based in space, the Strategic Defense Initiative, was nicknamed Star Wars. He tried to contain Communist spread in Latin America, sending military aid to the pro-American government of El Salvador and to rebels fighting Communist rule in Nicaragua. In 1983, he ordered the successful invasion of the Caribbean island of Grenada, where left-wing rebels had overthrown the government.

Many Americans liked Reagan's easy manner and felt he helped the nation "stand tall" in world affairs. In the 1984 presidential election, he won a record number of votes. In his second term, he met with Soviet leader Mikhail Gorbachev and agreed to reduce nuclear arms. In 1986, he bombed Libya to stop dictator Muammar el-Qaddafi from terrorist actions. It was a generally popular move, unlike the Iran-contra affair of the following year, when U.S. weapons were sold secretly to Iran to encourage release of American hostages. The money raised went to support contra rebels in Nicaragua. Later questioned about his involvement, Reagan answered, "I don't remember" 130 times.

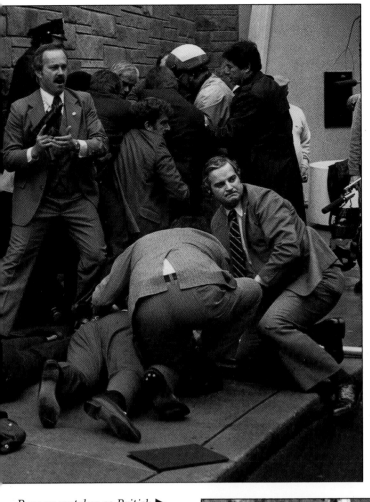

◀ *Just after Reagan is wounded in an assassination attempt in 1981, agents pin down the gunman at right, while others tend an aide who is badly hurt.*

▲ *Reagan and his wife, Nancy, also a former movie actor, enjoy a ride on their California ranch in 1980.*

Reagan watches as British ▶ *Prime Minister Margaret Thatcher reviews an honor guard on a Washington visit in 1988. Thatcher was one of Reagan's closest allies, and the "special relationship" between the U.S. and Great Britain flourished.*

◀ *As fearless flier Brass Bancroft, Ronald Reagan confronts Zelma, played by Rosella Towne, in* Secret Service of the Air, *a 1939 movie. Reagan made more than 50 movies, mostly westerns or action pictures.*

George Bush (1989–   )

George Herbert Walker Bush, 41st president, was born in Milton, Massachusetts, in 1924. During World War II, the teenage Bush became the U.S. Navy's youngest fighter pilot and was decorated for bravery in the Pacific. He then studied economics at Yale and entered the Texas oil industry, working his way up to company president.

Bush was elected to the U.S. House of Representatives in 1966 and served as U.S. ambassador to the United Nations. During the Watergate scandal, he was chairman of the Republican party and firmly supported Nixon to the end. In 1976, Bush served briefly as director of the Central Intelligence Agency (CIA), which was under much criticism. As Ronald Reagan's vice president, he was given unusual responsibility and, with the president's support, won a comfortable victory in the 1988 election.

In spite of an economic crisis and increasing national debt, Bush promised not to raise taxes. Problems at home were overshadowed by world events. In August 1990, Iraqi dictator Saddam Hussein invaded and occupied the Gulf state of Kuwait, a vital source of world oil. Bush had already taken a tough line in foreign affairs by ordering a brief invasion of Panama, and military intervention in the Philippines and Liberia. U.S. ground, air, and naval units became the major part of the half-million international troops sent to the Middle East.

On January 17, 1991, Bush authorized Operation Desert Storm, an all-out assault by U.S. and allied forces. The Iraqis were driven from Kuwait and forced to accept allied ceasefire terms on March 3. The Iraqis lost more than 100,000 men but killed fewer than 100 Americans. Bush was criticized for a delay in aiding thousands of Iraqi Kurds fleeing Saddam Hussein, and the dictator remained in power.

In the same period, the startling collapse of communism in Eastern Europe and rumbles of democracy in the Soviet Union offered hope for lasting peace. In 1991, the Soviet Union completely disintegrated, throwing the world situation into turmoil.

▲ In 1976, as director of the Central Intelligence Agency, Bush meets with Senator Church, in charge of a Senate investigation of CIA activities.

▼ In 1989, as communism crumbles in Eastern Europe, Bush is received with military honors by Polish leader General Wojciech Jaruzelski.

▲ George Bush poses for an official picture at the White House in front of the U.S. and presidential flags.

▼ The president and first lady wave good-bye after sharing Thanksgiving Day 1990 with U.S. Marines and British allies in Saudi Arabia.

▲ The Jefferson Memorial rises behind Bush and Soviet leader Mikhail Gorbachev, at ceremonies marking their Washington meeting in 1990.

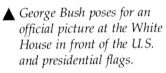

Further Reading about the Presidents of the United States

Beard, Charles A., and Detlev Vagts. *The Presidents in American History: George Washington to George Bush.* New York: Simon and Schuster, Inc., 1989.

Bourne, Russell, ed. *200 Years: A Bicentennial Illustrated History of the United States.* Vols. 1 and 2. Washington, D.C.: U.S. News and World Report, 1973.

Bowman, John. *A Pictorial History of the American Presidency.* New York: Gallery Books, 1991.

Burns, Roger. *George Washington.* New York: Chelsea House, 1987. (From the series *World Leaders Past and Present,* which also includes books on John Adams, John Quincy Adams, Dwight Eisenhower, Ulysses S. Grant, Alexander Hamilton, Andrew Jackson, Thomas Jefferson, Lyndon Johnson, John Kennedy, Abraham Lincoln, James Madison, James Monroe, Ronald Reagan, Franklin Roosevelt, Teddy Roosevelt, Harry Truman, and Woodrow Wilson.)

Chant, Christopher. *Presidents of the United States.* New York: Gallery Books, 1989.

Paletta, Lu Ann, and Fred L. Worth. *The World Almanac of Presidential Facts.* New York: Pharos Books, 1988.

Patrick, Sam J. *The Presidents: Washington to Bush.* Baltimore: Ottenheimer Publishers, Inc., 1989.

Post, Robert C., ed. *Every Four Years: The American Presidency.* Washington, D.C.: Smithsonian Exposition Books, 1980.

Provensen, Alice. *The Buck Stops Here: The Presidents of the United States.* New York: Harper and Row, 1990.

Wenborn, Neil, *The U.S.A.: A Chronicle in Pictures.* New York: Smithmark Publishers Inc., 1991.

Wright, John W., ed., *The Universal Almanac, 1992.* Kansas City, Mo.: Andrews and McMeel, 1991.

Picture Credits

Index

Adams, Abigail, 6, 7
Adams, John, 6–7, 8, 12
Adams, John Quincy, 11, 12–13
Adams, Louisa, 13
Agnew, Spiro, 56, 58
American Revolution, 4, 6, 8, 11, 15
Arthur, Chester A., 31

Blaine, James G., 30, 33
Booth, John Wilkes, 24, 25
Brown, John, 23
Bryan, William Jennings, 34, 38
Buchanan, James, 23
Bush, George, 62–63

Calhoun, John C., 11
Carter, James Earl, Jr., 59
Castro, Fidel, 51
Chou En-lai, 57
Churchill, Winston, 47
Civil War, 16, 21, 22, 23, 24, 26, 28, 29, 30, 33, 34
Clemenceau, Georges, 41
Cleveland, Esther, 32
Cleveland, Frances, 32
Cleveland, Grover, 32, 33

Conkling, Roscoe, 31
Constitution, U.S., 4, 10
Coolidge, Calvin, 38, 43, 44
Czolgosz, Leon, 34, 35

Declaration of Independence, 6, 8
Douglas, Stephen A., 24
Dulles, John Foster, 50

Edison, Thomas Alva, 29
Eisenhower, Dwight D., 50–51, 56

Fillmore, Millard, 21
Folsom, Frances, 32
Ford, Gerald R., Jr., 58
Ford, Henry, 33
Franklin, Benjamin, 8

Garfield, James, 30, 31
Goldwater, Barry, 54, 60
Gorbachev, Mikhail, 60, 63
Grant, Ulysses S., 28, 29, 38
Guiteau, Charles J., 30

Hanna, Marcus, 34

Harding, Warren G., 42, 43, 44
Harrison, Benjamin, 17, 33
Harrison, William Henry, 17, 18, 33
Hayes, Rutherford B., 29, 31, 34
Hoover, Herbert, 38, 44–45
Hussein, Saddam, 62

Irving, Washington, 10

Jackson, Andrew, 12, 13, 14–15, 16, 19
Jaruzelski, Wojciech, 62
Jefferson, Thomas, 6, 8–9, 10, 11, 12
Johnson, Andrew, 26–27
Johnson, Eliza, 26
Johnson, Lyndon B., 54–55

Kennedy, Edward, 52
Kennedy, Jacqueline, 52, 53
Kennedy, John, Jr., 53
Kennedy, John F., 52–53, 54, 56
Kennedy, Joseph P., 52
Kennedy, Robert, 52
Key, Francis Scott, 10

Khomeini, Ayatollah Ruhollah, 59
Khrushchev, Nikita, 50
Korean War, 48, 49, 50

Lee, Robert E., 24, 28
Lincoln, Abraham, 21, 23, 24–25, 26, 27, 28
Livingston, Robert, 8
Lloyd George, David, 41

MacArthur, Douglas, 48, 49
McCarthy, Joseph, 50
McClellan, George, 25
McKinley, William, 34–35, 36, 52
Madison, Dolley, 10
Madison, James, 10, 11
Mexican War, 19, 20, 22, 28
Monroe, James, 10, 11, 12
Montgomery, Bernard Law, 51
Morse, Samuel, 16

New Deal, 46, 48, 54
Nixon, Richard M., 52, 56–57, 58

Oswald, Lee Harvey, 52

Perry, Matthew, 22
Pierce, Franklin, 22
Polk, James Knox, 19, 23

Qaddafi, Muammar el-, 60

Reagan, Nancy, 61
Reagan, Ronald, 17, 60–61, 62
Roosevelt, Eleanor, 46, 47
Roosevelt, Franklin D., 38, 44, 46–47, 48, 54
Roosevelt, Quentin, 36
Roosevelt, Theodore, 35, 36–37, 38, 46, 52

Sadat, Anwar el-, 59
Scott, Dred, 23
Scott, Winfield, 19, 20, 22
Sherman, Roger, 8
Sinatra, Frank, 53
Spanish-American War, 34, 35, 36, 38
Stalin, Joseph, 47
Stanton, Edwin M., 27
Stevenson, Adlai, 50
Stowe, Harriet Beecher, 21

Taft, Robert, 38
Taft, William H., 38–39
Taylor, Zachary, 20, 21, 28
Thatcher, Margaret, 61
Tilden, Samuel J., 29
Truman, Bess, 49
Truman, Harry S, 48–49
Truman, Margaret, 49
Tyler, John, 18
Tyler, Julia, 18

United Nations, 49, 50, 62

Van Buren, Martin, 16, 17
Vietnam War, 52, 54, 55, 56, 58
Villa, Pancho, 40

War of 1812, 14, 17, 20
Washington, George, 4–5, 6, 8
Webster, Noah, 13
Wilson, Woodrow, 36, 38, 40–41
World War I, 40, 41, 42, 44
World War II, 44, 46, 48, 50